THE BABY
GUIDE

PRACTICAL ADVICE TO CALM OR TREAT
EXCESSIVE CRYING AND COLIC

Understand excessive crying
Why babies cry?
Find the right treatment
Soothing and coping techniques

1st Edition

MARK ANTHONY
&
FRANCESCA PROPHET

Copyright © 2016
Mark Anthony & Francesca Prophet
This book is sold subject to the condition that it shall not, by way of trade or otherwise, be lent, resold, hired out, or otherwise circulated without the publisher's prior consent in any form of binding or cover other than that in which it is published and without a similar condition including this condition being imposed on the subsequent publisher.
The moral right of Mark Anthony & Francesca Prophet has been asserted.
ISBN-13: 978-1539945666
ISBN-10: 1539945669

This book has not been created to be specific to any individual's or organizations' situation or needs. Every effort has been made to make this book as accurate as possible. This book should serve only as a general guide and not as the ultimate source of subject information. This book contains information that might be dated and is intended only to educate. The authors shall have no liability or responsibility to any person or entity regarding any loss or damage incurred, or alleged to have incurred, directly or indirectly, by the information contained in this book.

CONTENTS

Foreword 1

PART I. *Crying types* 2

   1. Normal crying 7
   2. Excessive crying 8

PART II. *Diagnosis* 9

   3. What 'dis-ease' does your baby have? 9

PART III. *Management of the conditions* 17

   4. Colic 17
   5. Reflux 28
   6. Cow's milk allergy (CMA) 41
   7. Trapped wind ('wind') 50
   8. Hunger and feeding difficulties 52
   9. Constipation 55
   10. Lactose intolerance 57
   11. Experimental approach to treating crying when the diagnosis is uncertain 60

PART IV. *Serious problems* 62

   12. Signs of serious illness 62

PART V. *What to do if your baby doesn't respond to treatment* .. 65

   13. Calming and soothing techniques 65
   14. Parental coping strategies 69

ACKNOWLEDGMENTS

We thank Christopher Prophet for his superb proof reading and grammar suggestions and all the parents with crying babies who have given us the insight and experience to write this book.

Foreword

Mark Anthony is a paediatrician and baby specialist. He has been a consultant neonatologist at the Newborn Intensive Care Unit, Oxford, UK for 10 years. He also sees parents and babies with colic and crying problems in Private Practice in Oxford. He is the father of four, one of whom had severe, classic colic, another severe reflux and two who cried normally.

Francesca Prophet is a neonatal nurse on the Newborn Intensive Care Unit, Oxford. She trained in Cape Town as a midwife and nurse, and has cared for parents and their newborn babies in South Africa and the UK for 15 years. She gives breast feeding advice and has an intimate understanding of crying babies and soothing techniques. She is known as 'the baby whisperer' when it comes to sleeping routines. Her son had severe reflux and hardly slept for the first three months.

This book has been written to help parents suffering the sleepless nights, stress and emotions associated with newborns who cry excessively. It is the work of two professionals who are themselves parents. The advice in this book is based on an understanding and thorough interpretation of the medical literature.

PART I

Crying types

A baby's cry causes stress in both parents. We are biologically designed to respond to crying and if our baby cannot be calmed, our parental stress and emotion levels rise. Parents become fraught, bicker, get exhausted and in extreme cases respond violently.

This book is designed to help parents with a baby who has 'excessive crying' – not the normal two hours per day spread over 24 hours, but the baby who cries with waking, cries until fed, cries intermittently during each feed, cries to sleep, sleeps short periods only and then cries again.

We will help you decide if your baby's crying is excessive, what the cause is, how to treat it and if no treatment helps, we offer some mechanisms to cope until the crying resolves over a few weeks to months – revealing the happy infant who's there to stay.

There is probably no relationship between excessive crying and cantankerous behaviour in childhood or later life. However, some studies suggest colic can influence parental perception of having a difficult child and adversely affect parent-child bonding.

All babies cry and some cry a lot. Crying is your baby's way of telling you he or she needs comfort and care – a way of communicating hunger, tiredness, boredom, overstimulation, wanting a cuddle, a wet nappy, being too hot or cold and later on, frustration. A normal cry starts off low pitched and grizzly and if ignored escalates to short spells of vigorous crying. As parents become experienced with their newborn over the first weeks, they become attuned to subtle differences in cries and begin to learn a tired cry is different from a hungry one.

Excessive crying is different – it can go on and on and on, with parents coming to understand, perhaps for the first time in their lives, what real exhaustion is like, from no break in the day and countless sleepless nights.

A view promoted by Sue Gerhardt (Why Love Matters) and Harvey Karp (The Happiest Baby on the Block) is that human babies, different from other baby mammals, are born as fetuses. They cannot focus their eyes and do not smile for weeks or move effectively for months. Karp describes the first three months of extrauterine life as the Fourth Trimester, born but not capable of doing much more than feed, and even this may be a challenge. As humans we've evolved to be born early because of our large brain size, unable to be delivered if we were born more mature.

The consequences of being born fetal are twofold:

- The brain is very immature, without emotional control and the ability to think.
- In the first few months babies prefer their world to be 'womb-like'.

Both these facts help us understand why Baby can be difficult in the first few months. Baby's crying has evolved as a survival mechanism. It is a reflex and we as parents have a built-in response. Some parents feel their baby dislikes them. Be reassured – the cry carries no personal vindication of you as a parent, it is simply a reflex. The parental response, however, means you cannot ignore the cry; and if the cry persists, your stress levels will rise.

Gerhardt and Karp argue convincingly that the solution to inconsolable crying is to provide love and a womb-like environment.

Gerhardt suggests that what starts out as a whimper can rapidly escalate to excessive crying because the higher cortical control of the deeper emotional brain is so under-developed. Once started, the brain activity that initiates a cry can easily explode into an electrical uncontrolled frenzy.

Providing a womb-like environment in the first three to four months helps prevent crying getting out of control and is the solution to calming Baby down again.

Several societies and racial groups do not have the problem of colic in their babies – colic does not exist. In these groups, Baby is usually carried almost all the time. It is close to mother day and night and feeding can be up to 100 times a day.

We think of ourselves as living in a sophisticated society but maybe we've got some things terribly wrong. A crying baby responds, as Karp describes, to the 5 'S's (swaddling, side or stomach lying, shushing, swinging, and sucking), all of which are most easily provided by being strapped to a parent. But what we often provide is back lying, sleeping in a bed away from Mother, and intermittent feeding – all potentially able to make Baby feel insecure and alone – a recipe for crying.

This book deals with the extreme. We presume by the time you've bought or borrowed this book you'll have been through all the normal soothing methods and are now desperate. The advice given here will help you decide whether to stick with soothing techniques or try medical treatments – which to try, and at what point to resign yourselves to waiting for the situation to naturally resolve itself. Even if you initiate medicines for the crying, don't give up on soothing techniques and trying to emulate the womb, especially in the first four months.

Some professionals use the terms 'excessive crying' and 'colic' interchangeably, but they are not the same. Excessive crying has several causes, only one of which is colic. Other reasons include gastroesophageal reflux ('reflux'), cow's milk allergy (CMA), lactose intolerance, trapped wind ('wind'), feeding difficulties leading to inadequate milk intake, hunger and constipation.

Unfortunately for parents and professionals, the signs and symptoms of these various conditions overlap and it can be a challenge to determine which one a baby has and, indeed, whether they have a condition at all. If the crying is abnormal, it's important to hone in on the exact diagnosis because the treatment is different depending on the condition.

Sometimes a diagnosis cannot be made or Baby is suffering from more than one condition, in which case a generic treatment strategy, covering several possibilities, may help. For a few babies no treatment works. Some paediatricians then label such babies as having behavioural crying.

Usually, though, there will be a cause, whether successfully identified or not. The good news is the causes are mostly benign and improve with age. When a diagnosis cannot be made and treatment doesn't work or takes time, this book gives strategies to help you, as parents, cope.

1. Normal crying

Some babies appear to be content with only the odd whine when hungry or needing a nappy change. Some don't cry much. In general, though, babies cry a lot during the first three months – an average of two hours a day – but with wide variation.

Some parents will consider crying for four hours as excessive. Others will treat it as normal.

By four months, babies cry on average an hour a day. Excessive crying is often defined as more than three hours. But it's not just the duration – the volume and pitch are also different from a normal cry.

Normal crying cues

Hunger: Mouth opening, rooting, fingers to lips, sticking tongue out, fidgeting

Sleepy: Rubbing eyes, yawning, blinking, staring, ear pulling, hiccups, gaze aversion

Too warm: Red face

Overstimulated: Intentionally turning away, gaze aversion, hiccups

Boredom: Escalating cry but settles when environment changed

Needing to poo: Grimacing, grunting, pushing

2. Excessive crying

Wessel in 1954 in a paper entitled 'Paroxysmal fussing in infancy, sometimes called colic' coined the Rule of Threes (Wessel Criteria) for classifying colic – crying for no apparent reason, for three or more hours per day, for three or more days per week, for more than three weeks in an otherwise healthy baby who is less than three months old.

Normal crying lasts less than two hours a day. Babies 'grizzle' when hungry, tired, bored or overstimulated. Loud, high-pitched, piercing crying is only an occasional feature. Excessively crying babies are wretched and cry most of the time, often with disturbed day and night sleep. The cry is high pitched, piercing and protracted. It grates and irritates.

An excessive cry is frequently accompanied with signs a baby is in pain. A starting point for dealing with this is to have confidence Baby does not have a serious disease (see Part four: Serious problems). A visit to a family doctor, general practitioner or paediatrician can be reassuring.

PART II

Diagnosis

3. What 'dis-ease' does your baby have?

We deal with the seven main causes of excessive crying – **colic** (paroxysmal pain in the evening), **reflux** (discomfort with vomiting), **CMA** (baby miserable and vomiting), **wind** (obvious relief with burping), **hunger**, **constipation**, and (rarely) **lactose intolerance**.

These conditions have overlapping symptoms and signs but with careful observation it's possible to identify the underlying cause. Decide for yourself which scenario best fits your baby.

IS IT COLIC?

- Sudden-onset, intense crying, usually in the evening
- Inconsolable
- Red in the face, angry, arms and legs tense, abdomen full
- No signs of disease
- Normal yellow stools (not green and no mucous or blood)
- No vomiting
- Baby is thriving
- Stops almost as suddenly as it starts and then Baby is happy
- Rule of threes
    - Three hours a day
    - Three times a week
    - Persists for more than three weeks
    - Self-resolves around three months (but can last six months)

IS IT REFLUX?

- Baby vomits, excessively possets or chews and gulps after feeds
- Crying coincides with vomiting or posseting
- Baby can be chronically irritable and unhappy
- Baby gags and brings milk into the mouth during and after feeds
- Feed aversion. On and off the teat/nipple because of hunger and pain (disturbed, uncomfortable feeder)
- Calm period for a few minutes after a feed, and then the crying starts
- Crying coincides with vomits
- Worse when lying flat, coupled with sleep disturbance
- Sometimes associated with respiratory symptoms
    - stridor (a high-pitched inspiratory noise)
    - wheeze
    - snuffliness/nasal congestion

- Baby is thriving (unless vomiting is so severe significant calories are lost) and there isn't a rash
- Parents or siblings may have had reflux as a baby

IS IT CMA?

- Baby miserable all the time
- Eczematous rash, facial redness or swelling around the eyes (sometimes anaphylactic reactions)
- Vomiting, reflux and feed aversion
- Green, mucousy and/or bloody stools and a sore bottom
- Occurs in breast-fed babies whose mothers are consuming cow's milk products
- Improves with a cow's milk free diet
- If formula milk feeding is changed to extensively hydrolysed formula (eHF) feeding, a dramatic improvement is seen
- Severe cases show failure to thrive
- Other family members have atopy, asthma or eczema

IS IT WIND?

- Baby draws in air with feeds. Makes clicking and sucking noises with feeding
- Difficult to 'burp' after feeding
- Bluish perioral tinge (grey-blue colour around the mouth) after feeds
- Upset towards the end and after feeds
- Lasts one to two hours or until Baby gives a big 'burp'
- May posset with burps but vomiting not a major issue
- Same pattern throughout 24 hours, not increasing towards the evening
- Passes lots of wind
- Gurgling in the abdomen
- No failure to thrive; normal stools; no rash

IS IT CONSTIPATION?

- Not usually associated with breast feeding
- Occurs with formula feeding, Gaviscon and thickeners (hence may be a complication of reflux treatment)
- Stools changed in consistency, colour and frequency
- Firm, infrequent stools
- Baby red in the face and straining, then relieved when passes a stool

IS IT LACTOSE INTOLERANCE?

- Rare as a primary severe deficiency
- Mild deficiency is common in children/adults but not in babies
- Distended, noisy abdomen
- Frothy stools and sore bottom
- Family history of lactose intolerance
- May improve with lactase drops

IS IT HUNGER?

- Feeding never properly established (mother on the verge of giving up breast feeding)
- Baby cries after feeds, mouthing and looking for more food
- Growth faltering/failure to thrive
- Green, loose stools but not frothy. No mucous or blood
- No rash
- When fed more, Baby settles beautifully

PART III

Management of the conditions

4. Colic

Up to a quarter of all babies suffer from colic, a challenging condition for parents and professionals.

Although the term colic is used for persistent crying, it's a specific condition of unknown cause with a characteristic pattern of paroxysms of sudden, high-pitched crying, often in the evening and lasting more than three hours. It starts when Baby is a few weeks old. The crying is louder and more high-pitched than crying for other reasons. Baby appears to be in pain – red in the face, legs drawn up, tense abdomen, back arched, and stiff arms and legs.

Colic disappears after a few hours, almost as suddenly as it started. Baby then appears to be entirely well. Colic is not associated with vomiting, Baby is thriving and stools are normal.

Colic is not a sign of underlying serious disease. No baby has died from it, except the few who suffer non-accidental injury from over-stressed and exhausted parents. Studies suggest colic is not an early indicator of a child who is going to be 'difficult', or shape one into being more unhappy or sensitive. In fact, colic has no direct relationship with any later behaviour in the child.

It may influence the child in an indirect way – the early excessive screaming may alter the parent-baby bonding. This sometimes has long-lasting consequences for the happiness of the parent and the attachment of the child. Exhausted parents must remember however bad it may seem at the time, the screaming will resolve after three or four months, perhaps after treatment.

A few months will seem like a long way away when Baby is only four weeks old and you've already had enough. But see Part Five, especially 'parental coping strategies', and keep in mind that a normal, happy infant will eventually emerge from your screaming and miserable bundle.

The UK National Institute of Health and Clinical Excellence recommends reassuring parents their baby is well, that they are not doing something wrong and the baby is not rejecting them. Colic is common and will resolve itself. Colic is a self-limiting condition, with crying significantly improving in 60 percent of three-month-olds and 90 percent of four-month-olds.

The bad news is there appears to be no instant medical cure – to be frank one must simply cope until the colic resolves itself.

Why does colic occur?

We don't know. It may be due to immature gut motility, trapped wind, gas development within the lumen of the gut or abnormal gut bacterial flora (hence the rationale for using probiotics). And, a proportion of colic is actually misdiagnosed CMA.

Is there any treatment that can help?
Probiotics

Probiotics may be beneficial, especially those containing *Lactobacillus reuterii*. The best studies indicate there is a benefit only if the probiotic is started soon after birth, before colic has developed.

Other studies hint at an improvement in crying when probiotics are started around the time of onset of colic. Probiotics can sometimes make Baby vomit, have loose stools, cause a rash and exacerbate crying.

If you are going to try probiotics, use them as early as possible and consider lowering the dosage from that suggested on the packet. If there is no clear benefit, stop using them.

Probiotics do appear to be safe – given to preterm babies from birth, studies indicate they prevent necrotising enterocolitis (a serious inflammatory gut condition only seen in preterm babies). There are virtually no side effects. Extrapolating this experience from premature babies to babies born at term, a trial for a short period may help colic without any serious consequence.

Avoidance of cow's milk protein (CMP)

Some colic responds to removal of CMP and some is misdiagnosed, being actually cow's milk allergy (CMA). Either way, a CMP-free diet may help.

If Mother is solely breast feeding, CMPs can be transmitted through the breast milk to Baby. Mother must avoid foods containing CMP and this means giving up milk and dairy products – no milk in tea and coffee, no butter, no cake made with milk or butter, and no cheese.

We suggest Mother tries CMP avoidance in this way. If no clear and significant improvement is seen in Baby, she should start drinking milk again for her own health.

Soya protein intolerance occurs in 30 percent of babies who have CMA, so mothers may also want to avoid soya protein in their diet. We don't recommend this more extreme dietary restriction unless there is good evidence the crying is CMA rather than colic-related. It is difficult to avoid both cow's milk and soya in a mother's diet, and conversely there is some evidence soya milk may actually improve colic.

In formula-fed babies with colic, extensively hydrolysed formula (eHF) may be the answer (see chapter on CMA for the various brands available). Try an eHF if the diagnosis is CMA. There will usually be an improvement within two days. If there is no improvement and it is challenging to get Baby to drink the eHF, then abandon the trial.

If there is some improvement but Baby refuses to feed, then consider switching between eHFs until you find one Baby tolerates. For taste and cost reasons, you should resume Baby's original (non-hydrolysed) formula if there is no improvement.

Maternal colic diets

There is evidence maternal colic diets improve a crying situation. Lust, in 1996, looked at colic in almost 300 breastfed infants and found that cow's milk, cabbage, cauliflower, broccoli, onion and chocolate were associated with colic. Other studies also hint at curry, citrus fruit, caffeine and alcohol as possible causes.

Garlic, green peppers, orange juice, Brussels sprouts, dried beans, eggs, carrots, beef and beer were not linked to colic.

Hill showed in 2005 that a low-allergen diet, avoiding wheat, cow's milk, soya, eggs, peanuts and fish, dramatically reduced colic. A cow's milk free diet, or a colic diet if there's a family history of coeliac, atopy, asthma or eczema, could be tried.

If there is no improvement, quickly abandon and be careful not to over restrict mother's diet.

Soya milk

In contrast to the exclusion of soya, some studies of colic suggest symptoms improve with feeding a soya-based formula. The jury is still out on the subject but almost all professionals now advise against feeding babies soya milk. This is because of the high levels of phytoestrogens and the unknown hormonal influence this might have on future reproductive organ development.

The concern is that if a baby is drinking only soya milk, its small body size compared to adults makes for a much higher intake of phytoestrogens. In the UK, soya-based formula, such as SMA Wysoy, is reserved for babies with a rare metabolic condition known as galactosaemia, for babies of vegans (when Mother cannot breast feed), and occasionally for babies with CMA when Baby refuses to drink eHF.

So if you are formula feeding your baby and you're going to change Baby's diet for colic reasons, the first choice should be eHF, the second a different eHF, and lastly a soya-based formula. If no benefit is seen, swap back to the original milk.

Soya milks contain higher concentrations of glucose and can cause decay in baby teeth.

Herbal teas

Some studies suggest herbal teas may be beneficial for colic but there is an issue with the regulation of herbal products – all the ingredients are not necessarily written on the box; some teas include low doses of poisonous ingredients (anise tea, for instance, contains star of anise which can be neurotoxic); and the manufacturing process may mean there is bacterial contamination. Karp proposes a trial of tea made with fennel or dill seeds – a few crushed seeds, steeped in boiling water, cooled and then given as a teaspoonful a few times a day.

Colic Calm (www.coliccalm.co.uk) is a commercial herbal remedy and appears to be successful for some babies with colic. It contains amongst other herbs fennel, caraway, chamomile, ginger and mint.

Infacol (simethicone)

Simethicone is thought to work by encouraging gas bubbles to enlarge so they can then be expelled by 'burping'. There is no evidence that simethicone works, but as there is an overlap between colic and trapped wind, a trial of simethicone in combination with efforts to effectively wind/burp Baby after each feed is worthwhile. Simethicone interrupts the absorption of thyroxine, so don't give it in the rare event your baby has congenital hypothyroidism.

Milk preincubated with lactase

Lactase and simethicone are the only treatments suggested by the UK National Institute of Health and Clinical Excellence (NICE) for colic – weak evidence suggests that in some babies preincubating milk with lactase drops may help. The treatment is inexpensive and can be stopped if no benefit is seen.

If Baby shows some improvement, stop the drops at three to six months old. True lactase deficiency is rare but, nevertheless, some babies seem to respond to lactase drops.

Dicycloverine

In adults, dicycloverine (also known as dicyclomine) is used for irritable bowel syndrome. It works by blocking cholinergic receptors and thereby relaxing intestinal smooth muscle, hence reducing cramps and spasms.

Side effects include dry mouth, nausea and euphoria. High doses can cause delirium.

A few trials of dicycloverine show it improves crying. In one study, colic was cured in almost two thirds of infants, compared with a quarter given placebo. But, one in twelve babies given dicycloverine have side effects such as drowsiness, constipation and diarrhoea.

Occasional severe side effects have also been noted, including pauses in breathing, fits and coma. Infants six weeks old and less are most vulnerable to severe reactions. Some professionals argue that the beneficial effects of dicycloverine outweigh the relatively low incidence of adverse effects. But the manufacturer now advises against its use in infants under six months.

Perhaps closely supervised use in babies over two months old may be beneficial but this requires the cooperation of a doctor prepared to prescribe the drug for an unlicensed indication.

The UK NHS Choices website includes dicycloverine as a treatment to avoid because of the possibility of serious side effects.

Hyoscine

Hyoscine hydrobromide (also known as scopolamine; brand names Buscopan and Hyospasmol) is an anti-cholinergic drug with anti-spasmodic properties. Theoretically it could relieve colic. Common side effects include drowsiness, reduced ability to sweat, fast and then slow heart rate and itching. Rarely, it can cause hallucinations, agitation and fits.

Feeding techniques

Hints Baby is not feeding correctly are clicks and drawing in of air, excess wind (needing lots of burping before settling after a feed) and passing wind below (flatus). In extreme cases, Baby is hungry most of the time and may be failing to thrive. If Baby is not feeding and being burped effectively, these may be the cause of the crying (see Hunger and Wind).

Colic bottles

Try a different bottle, especially those designed to let in air other than through the teat (Mam and Dr Brown are good examples). Check the size of the teat hole and change the size if necessary (smaller if Baby is choking on milk; larger if Baby is drawing in air).

Offer bottles more frequently for a few days. If there's a lot of crying during a feed, the baby isn't hungry yet or has simply become too stressed, leave for half an hour and then try again.

Early weaning is not helpful

Weaning should commence at around six months. Early weaning should start at four months, not earlier. Colic should self-resolve in the majority of babies by the time early weaning starts; and weaning is not thought to be beneficial for colic.

Colic facts

- Colic is common and resolves on its own after three or four months
- Baby does not have a serious disease
- As parents, you are doing nothing wrong
- Colic is not a sign Baby is rejecting you
- You are not alone – it happens to all sorts of parents (including one of the authors)
- Soothing and coping techniques are the mainstay of managing the problem
- Involve friends, grandparents, relatives and anyone else who can take Baby for short periods to give you a break
- Take it in turns to soothe Baby
- Look for other parents with a colicky baby and share your experiences
- Parental feelings of exhaustion, anger, frustration, helplessness and guilt are all normal responses to incessant crying – remember it's only for a few weeks

Colic management
First line interventions

- Simethicone, lactase and herbal remedies (unlikely to work but cheap and harmless)
- Focus on feeding and winding techniques
- Introduce probiotics (cheap and possibly beneficial)

- Reconsider the diagnosis. Could it be reflux or CMA?
- Colic bottle (like Mam or Dr Brown)

Second line

- Breast feeding
  - Maternal avoidance of cow's milk
  - Maternal 'colic' diet if family history of food intolerance exists
- Formula feeding
  - eHF
  - Soya formula if baby refuses eHF

Complementary approach

- Soothing techniques
- Parental coping strategies

5. Reflux

'Reflux' is an abbreviation for 'gastroesophageal reflux' – the return of gastric contents into the oesophagus from the stomach, causing heartburn, regurgitation and in severe cases vomiting.

Reflux occurs because of relaxation in the lower oesophageal sphincter, the ring of muscle that releases and constricts to let food into the stomach. The sphincter is looser in babies and reflux is more likely to occur when lying on the back. Like colic, it's a self-resolving condition, but reflux can last longer than colic. Conversely, reflux is more effectively treated than colic.

'Happy spitters' refers to a group of babies who have uncomplicated reflux – that which does not cause discomfort. Baby can feed well and is thriving. More than half of all four-month-olds show some degree of regurgitation of milk but most have uncomplicated reflux that causes no discomfort or respiratory or feeding problems.

Reflux becomes 'reflux disease' when it causes discomfort, respiratory problems (stridor and wheeze) and in severe cases failure to thrive (so much milk is expelled calorie intake is insufficient for growth).

Babies with reflux disease often appear to have feed aversion – they pull away from the breast or bottle, sometimes choking on the milk and appear to be in pain. Such babies can take one or more hours to feed and have hardly settled before crying for the next feed. Most babies should complete a feed in fifteen to twenty minutes; if it takes more than twenty-five minutes, reflux may be the issue.

Babies with reflux disease posset more than their peers, have frequent frank vomiting, hiccup often, are disturbed and uncomfortable feeders (pulling away from the breast or bottle, are agitated and may appear to have a swallowing difficulty or feed aversion), can be chronically irritable and unhappy, get worse when laid flat on their backs, have sleep disturbance, and nasal congestion, wheezing and/or a high-pitched inspiratory cry. Babies with bad reflux sleep badly.

Reflux can run in families, having occurred in siblings or parents when they were babies. Sandifer Syndrome is the name given to arching of the back, torsion of the neck and chin lifting from severe reflux disease. Reflux naturally resolves itself in more than half of babies within ten months. By 18 months 80 percent are cured, and almost all by two years.

What treatments help?

If you're reading this book, it is more likely your baby has reflux disease rather than being a happy spitter. You should though consider whether the symptoms are tolerable and whether you really want to embark on treatment.

Watch Baby carefully and decide whether the crying episodes coincide with regurgitation of milk; it may not be obvious but tell-tale signs are facial grimacing, swallowing, chewing, and some milk in the mouth. Treating reflux disease in babies can be difficult; what works for one may not work for another.

Tests

Tests for reflux are difficult to perform and often give inconclusive results. Endoscopies, barium meal x-rays and pH probes are invasive and should not be undertaken lightly. In general, for babies with reflux as a cause of excessive crying the diagnosis is a clinical one and no testing is required or particularly helpful.

In our practice we reserve tests for those with more severe presentation and symptoms persisting beyond a year of age. If a young baby has sufficiently severe vomiting it fails to thrive or the vomiting is projectile, it may be wise to rule out pyloric stenosis with an abdominal ultrasound scan.

Positioning when lying down

An 18-degree slope under a cot mattress and left lateral or prone lying can reduce reflux for mechanical reasons. The lower oesophageal sphincter lies to the right and posterior to the stomach, hence the left lateral and prone (front sleeping) positions help to keep milk away from the lower oesophagus.

Prone and lateral positioning are, however, no longer recommended for normal sleeping babies because of the association with sudden infant death syndrome (SIDS). These positions are occasionally still recommended for severe reflux, but studies of their effectiveness have shown mixed results. Given the association with SIDS, you may want to prioritise head-up positioning and other interventions before prone and left lateral sleeping.

An 18-degree angle may not be sufficient for bad reflux but is about the maximum slope a baby can easily lie in without slipping to the foot of the bed. If the reflux is severe, consider a steeper wedge with a fastening mechanism to keep Baby in place, such as the BabyB brand.

Positioning when feeding

Feed Baby in an upright position as much as possible, such as the vertical latch technique for breast feeding. Bottle feeding can also be done with both Baby vertical and the bottle upright. Aim to keep Baby vertical for about 20 minutes after a feed before putting him down for a post-prandial snooze.

The BabyB Brand bean bag may be helpful. (www.babybbrand.com)

Cow's milk free diet

Up to 40 percent of babies with reflux have underlying intestinal inflammation from cow's milk allergy (CMA). Less frequently there are other dietary protein intolerances. If possible, maternal avoidance of cow's milk protein (CMP) or a more extensive hypoallergenic diet (avoiding CMP, soya, nuts, eggs and wheat) for the breast-fed baby, or a trial of extensively hydrolysed formula (eHF) for a formula-fed baby. This single intervention may produce a dramatic change in reflux symptoms.

A baby with CMA will normally have other signs of disease – mucous and/or blood in stools or rectal bleeding, eczematous rash, failure to thrive and constant misery. Some family members may also have had CMA as a baby (whether diagnosed or not).

Others in the family may suffer atopy – eczema and/or asthma.

If your baby has symptoms of CMA, see the section on CMA. About 30 percent of babies with CMA also have soya intolerance.

Mucosal barrier agents

Gaviscon has a good safety profile in babies and is known to aid reflux. It is not an antacid, however, and partial improvement in vomiting may not be associated with a reduction in crying.

Gaviscon is often prescribed with an antacid such as the H2 antagonist, ranitidine. Gaviscon can be given prior to or after a feed, on a spoon mixed with a little milk or water or added to formula milk or expressed breast milk.

Feed thickeners

Feed thickening can dramatically reduce reflux but for many babies it only brings about a modest improvement and at a cost of causing constipation. Thickening is relatively harmless and should be the first-line approach before using anti-reflux medication.

Thickening agents include oat cereal, rice starch, maize starch, carob flour and locust bean gum. Xanthan gum is no longer recommended as a thickener because it may occasionally cause serious intestinal inflammation. Cereals used to thicken milk increase the calories by up to 1 kcal/ml and so should be avoided in overweight babies. Gluten-containing cereals should be avoided as a thickener for babies born to a family with coeliac disease.

Thickeners can be added to 30 ml expressed milk at the start of a feed using a bottle or Dinky feeder. You may have to widen the teat. Don't listen to advice about not mixing breast and bottle feeding. It is more important to try to ease the reflux.

Anti-reflux milks such as Enfamil AR (containing rice starch), Aptamil Anti-Reflux (carob bean gum), Aptamil Comfort (potato and maize starch) and SMA Stay Down (maize starch) are available for formula-fed babies.

All thickening agents, with the exception of carob (i.e. Carobel), require stomach acidity to activate the thickener and so antacids such as H2s and PPIs (see below) should not be prescribed for a baby who is taking a thickened formula milk. Some doctors do, however, co-prescribe antacids and thickened formula and parental reports suggest that the combination does still work.

Carobel is added to a bottle and over ~5 minutes thickens the milk prior to feeding. The next size up teat or a variflow teat is required to ensure that Baby can suck the thickened milk from the bottle. Half a scoop is added to every 90 ml (thin) or a whole scoop (thick) to every 60 ml milk.

If breast feeding, you should not switch to formula milk for the purpose of thickening, especially as so many babies with apparent reflux actually have underlying CMA. Also, breast milk has a protective effect against reflux, possibly because of stimulation of pro-kinetic gut hormones.

Medications

Acid reflux causes inflammation and pain in the lower oesophagus and worsens the laxity of the lower oesophageal sphincter, exacerbating the condition. However, medication is not recommended for uncomplicated reflux because it probably isn't the cause of the excessive crying. There are also minor safety concerns with anti-reflux drugs and the problem will mostly self-resolve.

When other techniques fail, medication is warranted for babies with excessive crying caused by reflux. If a treatment is found to be effective, consider stopping it at one to two monthly intervals after three months, until it can be stopped without recurrence of the discomfort. The two main groups of drugs used for reflux disease are H2-antagonists (H2s) and proton pump inhibitors (PPIs).

Histamine2-receptor antagonists (H2s)

The H2 drugs block acid secretion in the stomach. H2s are typified by ranitidine, the only drug in the H2 group routinely used for babies. It has a high safety profile for short-term use.

H2s have been around longer than PPIs and are sometimes prescribed as the initial drug of choice; more for reasons to do with doctor familiarity and possibly less side effects, not because they are more effective.

Proton pump inhibitors (PPIs)

The PPIs commonly prescribed for babies are

omeprazole, lansoprazole and esomeprazole – there is no good evidence of one being more effective than another for baby reflux and until evidence is available the authors' preferred choice is omeprazole. They act by blocking the biochemical pump that secretes acid into the stomach. PPIs are the most effective medical treatment for baby reflux disease, especially that causing excessive crying. Some argue PPIs are the only effective and safe medication for the condition.

For omeprazole, a usual infant dose is 1-2 mg/kg/day. If this proves ineffective up to 3 mg/kg/day (total daily dose 20 mg) can be given. A measure of being on the edge of the effective therapeutic dose is when a delayed or missed dose leads to recurrence of the crying and vomiting.

No drug is without side effects and long-term potential risks of omeprazole include increased risk of acquiring pneumonia and diarrhoea, B12 and iron deficiency and osteoporosis (bone thinning). However, the experience of about 20 years of short-term use in babies shows that PPIs are safe and have few side effects. Some babies have an increase in colicky symptoms for a few days after commencing a PPI, so it is worthwhile persisting for at least a week once the decision has been made to initiate treatment.

Stopping a PPI can lead to rebound hypersecretion of acid for a few days. If there is a revival of symptoms after stopping you should wait for several days before deciding to resume the therapy.

H2 versus PPI

Omeprazole is better at reducing acidity and crying

episodes than ranitidine. But there is much more experience of using ranitidine in babies.

Depending on the severity of your baby's crying your doctor may initially prescribe a H2 drug. If not effective, he might prescribe a PPI (the step-up approach).

If by the time you seek help the screaming is severe, your doctor may start with a PPI. Once the reflux is well controlled he may then advise changing to ranitidine (the step-down approach).

Where reflux is the cause of excessive crying there is a good argument for starting promptly with a PPI, as a diagnostic process as well as treatment. If there is a sudden, dramatic improvement then the diagnosis is clear – this may take a few days to materialise and necessitate increasing the dose to 3 mg/kg/day (maximum total daily dose of 20 mg).

Crying is likely to resolve over a few months as Baby grows, hence the PPI will be only used short-term. Even if the reflux persists the crying component may reduce, allowing the PPI to be stopped or stepped down to ranitidine.

As a rough guide, if a PPI is started at two to three months and can be stopped before eight months, then this brief use warrants staying on the PPI and not switching to a H2. If the early presentation leads to persisting reflux, and the use of the PPI is drifting into long-term use, say beyond ten to twelve months, then depending on the severity of the persisting symptoms we consider switching to ranitidine. This is a decision to be made with your doctor.

When switching from H2 to PPI, the H2 interferes

with the mechanism of action of the PPI (drug interaction) and can make the PPI ineffective. Either stop the H2 for a day and start the PPI the next and risk an exacerbation of the symptoms for one to three days as the PPI builds up in the system, or overlap the two drugs for a few days, in which case give the PPI first and the H2 more than four hours later in the day.

Prokinetics

This group of drugs work for some babies but not others. If PPIs are not fully effective then consider a trial of a prokinetic as an additional agent. But first take time to experiment with increasing PPI doses.

Metaclopramide

Metaclopramide has a long history of safe use in babies but can cause tiredness, sleeplessness and irritability and on rare occasions dystonic reactions (arching, head turning, dramatic posturing). This requires an antidote (diphenhydramine).

Given the potential for frequent irritability/sleep problems and rare dystonic reactions, this drug has been superseded by domperidone.

Domperidone

Domperidone is a dopamine receptor antagonist and increases peristalsis and gastric emptying. Studies show only modest reduction in reflux symptoms and these can take over four weeks to become evident. The UK Medicines and Healthcare products Regulatory Agency (MHRA) advises against giving domperidone to children for reflux or heartburn because of a risk of heart rhythm disturbances – seen occasionally in adults taking this drug for prolonged periods.

In the UK domperidone is still indicated for nausea and vomiting in children but only for a maximum duration of a week. Given the potential cardiac risk and only modest effectiveness, H2 and PPIs are the preferred drugs, leaving domperidone as a supplement to PPIs in severe cases. Side effects include diarrhoea, lactation and sleepiness.

Cisapride

This is a selective serotonin agonist that increases intestinal motility. It is no longer recommended for babies as it has been associated with heart rhythm disturbance and occasionally sudden death in adults.

Does weaning help?

Weaning onto solids can initially make reflux worse. Some babies do improve with weaning as solids act in the same way as thickeners. It may take time to see a response. Weaning when it does help is usually not a magic bullet, some improvement but no cure.

Burping

Ineffective burping exacerbates reflux and is just another cause of discomfort. See section on trapped wind and 'burping' techniques.

Surgery

Very occasionally, medications are not enough to control the reflux. In severe cases, a surgeon will consider an operation to tighten the oesophageal sphincter if there are life-threatening aspiration events (milk and acid refluxing into the lungs), severe respiratory symptoms, and/or failure to thrive. Surgery will not usually be considered until Baby is over one year old.

There are risks to any operation and surgery should not be undertaken lightly. Sometimes the side effects from surgery, such as gas trapping/wind, can be worse than the original reflux symptoms. Consequently, surgery does not have a role in treating reflux that is causing excessive crying in young babies.

Approach to trying different strategies

Switching between treatments and strategies too quickly can leave everyone confused, never quite knowing whether there was a temporary improvement or if the intervention worked. Choose a paediatrician or family doctor who is comfortable with crying babies, and let them help you in the process of treatment.

Reflux management

Level 1   Positioning is paramount 18- to 30-degree slope to bed and changing mat
Focus on winding technique
Simethicone, Gaviscon & ranitidine

Level 2 Complete maternal avoidance of CMP, if breast fed
eHF, if formula fed
Level 3 PPI. Start with omeprazole. If this is ineffective consider esomeprazole and/or lansoprazole
Level 4 Domperidone
Refer to a paediatric gastroenterologist

Reflux facts

- Better known as gastroesophageal reflux
- Self-resolving condition
  - Resolves in >50% by 10 months
  - 80 percent by 18 months
  - 98 percent by 24 months
- 'Happy spitters' have uncomplicated reflux not requiring treatment
- Reflux disease is complicated by pain, respiratory symptoms and failure to thrive
- Reflux disease is associated with feed aversion
- Feeding takes 15 to 20 minutes; if more than 25 minutes reflux may be the issue.
- Babies with reflux disease have sleep disturbance
- Reflux can run in families

6. Cow's milk allergy (CMA)

CMA is an abnormal immune response to cow's milk protein (CMP) in the gut.

This aberrant immune reaction causes inflammation in the intestines from stomach to colon. The inflammation in turn causes abnormal peristalsis, discomfort and malabsorption of digested milk. It occurs in about 3 percent of formula-fed babies and 0.5 to 1 percent of those that are breast fed. CMPs can pass through Mother to Baby in breast milk.

Babies with CMA are miserable most of the time and may be worse soon after a feed. They may vomit (the inflammation of the gut causes reflux) and stools may be loose, containing mucous and/or blood. There is likely to be an eczematous-like rash and possibly urticaria, facial redness and/or periorbital oedema (inflammation is not restricted to the gut; there is a generalised immune overreaction with dermatological consequences).

Some babies with CMA have respiratory symptoms (nasal congestion/snuffliness, wheezing and stridor) and they may fail to thrive.

Colic, reflux, hunger and CMA all cause severe crying but CMA has the greatest systemic impact. Babies with CMA tend to be miserable between crying episodes.

Two forms of CMA have been identified: *IgE-* and

non-IgE-mediated. The former causes reactions to cow's milk within minutes; the latter produces symptoms from two to 72 hours. When treated by CMP-avoidance the change from a despondent and wretched baby to a happy one can be dramatic. For *IgE-mediated* disease the change can occur within 24 hours (slower, over a few days, for *non-IgE-mediated*).

In the families of babies with CMA there tend to be others with atopic illness – asthma, eczema and allergies.

The UK MAP (Milk Allergy in Primary care) guideline divides CMA into four categories:

Mild-moderate non-IgE-mediated CMA (delayed onset; two to 72 hours)

Abdominal discomfort and vomiting that imitate colic and reflux, with milk refusal or aversion, loose and frequent stools, perianal redness, constipation, blood and/or mucous in stools in an otherwise well baby. Other symptoms are itching, skin erythema or frank eczema, nasal snuffles, stridor or wheezing.

Severe non-IgE-mediated CMA (delayed onset; two to 72 hours)

Diarrhoea, vomiting, abdominal pain, food refusal and aversion, significant blood/mucous in irregular or uncomfortable stools, failure to thrive (weight loss, or gaining weight but not following weight percentile) and severe atopic eczema.

Mild-moderate IgE-mediated CMA (acute onset; within minutes)

Acute itching, erythema, urticarial and/or oedema, vomiting, diarrhoea, abdominal pain (suggestive of colic), rhinitis and/or conjunctivitis.

Severe IgE-mediated CMA (anaphylactic reaction)

Immediate reaction to milk exposure, with severe respiratory symptoms, weak pulse and hypotension. It is a rare but potentially life-threatening reaction, necessitating initial emergency resuscitation/stabilisation and hospital admission.

The challenge with CMA is that it is a diverse disease with severity ranging from mild to extreme, depending on the baby. The symptoms, especially when dealing with the milder end of the CMA spectrum, can be difficult to differentiate from reflux and colic. In fact up to 40 percent of babies diagnosed with reflux probably have underlying CMA.

Diagnosis

The diagnosis of CMA is a clinical one – that is to say there is no good test to definitively say a baby has the illness or not. It can be difficult for parents to be objective about whether an improvement has occurred with CMP-avoidance or to differentiate one cause of crying from another.

For this reason, it is wise to involve a paediatrician or family doctor – someone who isn't caught up in the cycle of tiredness and exhaustion. Someone who can be objective and slow down the process of switching too rapidly from one treatment to another, desperately looking for a quick cure.

IgE testing can be offered to help distinguish between the IgE- and non-IgE-mediated forms of CMA, as the category of disease influences the decision and mode of reintroduction of milk into the infant diet.

The most useful IgE tests are skin prick (undertaken in an allergy centre, not in a community clinic (in case of anaphylaxis) or antibody blood test (can be done in the clinic if there is the expertise to obtain blood from a young baby).

Atopy patch testing and oral food challenges to diagnose IgE-mediated food allergy should not be done in primary care or community settings.

Management

The treatment of CMA is simple avoidance of CMP in all its forms. In the UK it's estimated over 18,000 infants a year are prescribed extensively hydrolysed (eHF) or amino acid (AAF) formulas for CMA, at a cost of £25 million a year.

The treatment for breast-fed babies is cheaper but possibly more inconvenient – maternal avoidance of all CMP. No cow's milk for Mother means no milk, no butter or cheese, and none of the ready-made meals containing milk products. All these foods have to be omitted from the diet for the duration of breast feeding or until Baby is around a year old.

Management of the formula-fed baby is a

challenge because of eHF/AAFs aren't as palatable as standard cow's milk formula. The hydrolysis process for eHFs involves breakdown of proteins into peptides, whereas AAFs are completely artificial milks built from basic amino acids, lipid and carbohydrate constituents.

The taste issue means some babies adamantly refuse to drink eHF/AAFs; conversely some babies with severe CMA quickly associate the new taste with feeling better and tolerate the milk well.

If Baby is breast milk fed, the treatment for all four categories of CMA is complete maternal CMP avoidance. If Baby is formula fed, use eHF for mild-moderate CMA. If Baby refuses to drink eHF switch formulas until you find one that works. The authors use eHF for all but the most severe forms of CMA, for which AAF is given. When an AAF is prescribed this is usually in conjunction with making a referral to a paediatric gastroenterologist.

Maternal complete CMP-avoidance

If after a 1-2 week trial period, complete maternal CMP-avoidance is successful in improving Baby's crying, continue the maternal dietary restriction – potentially for a year and occasionally beyond. Mother should be prescribed vitamin D and calcium supplements, and be referred to a dietician.

Some eHFs can be purchased without a prescription but are often expensive. If you live in a country where special formula milks are provided on prescription and are free at the point of use, it may still be worthwhile initially buying a selection so you can rapidly assess each for palatability (without having to make a doctor's appointment each time you want to try another brand). When you have decided on the best eHF for your baby you can obtain future supplies on prescription.

Uncertain diagnosis at the start

At times, it's not clear whether a baby has CMA or some other cause of excessive crying. The process of trying to feed a baby eHF, especially when the diagnosis is uncertain, can be difficult. Many babies with colic and many with reflux do, however, have underlying CMA. So if there is even a small chance of the diagnosis being CMA, it's worth persevering with the decision to use an eHF (using an AAF is not appropriate if the diagnosis of CMA is uncertain).

Babies who fall into the mild-moderate non-IgE-mediated CMA group and have responded to eHF/AAFs or maternal CMP-free diet are usually maintained CMP-free until 9 to 12 months. Milk is introduced slowly in cooked form as part of the solids diet – starting with malted milk biscuits, then digestive biscuits, then muffins, pancakes, shepherd's pie, lasagne, pizza, milk chocolate buttons, yoghurt, cheddar cheese, and finally infant formula milk. See the MAP Milk Ladder

(http://cowsmilkallergyguidelines.co.uk).

Overall, 50 percent of CMA cases have resolved themselves within a year, 75 percent by three years, and 90 percent by six years. If the symptoms return with reintroduction of CMP then you should continue to restrict the diet.

Reintroducing milk for infants with severe non-IgE-mediated CMA or any form of IgE-mediated CMA should be done with the guidance of an allergy specialist and in a place of safety, in case of anaphylaxis.

Case Histories

Maisy

Maisy was solely breastfed from birth and started copious vomiting at two weeks old. She also had evening colic - inconsolable high-pitched screaming from 5 pm which stopped as abruptly as it started at 10 pm. She had normal stools, no rash and was growing well.

By the time Maisy was four weeks old her mother was eating a 'colic' diet, and had tried simethicone and colic calm. Simethicone had no effect on the colic or the vomiting. Colic Calm worked amazingly for the colic, but only for two minutes. Maisy developed a faint rash on her back and abdomen, thought by parents to be a heat rash as it was early summer.

Mother changed her diet to exclude cow's milk protein - she did not eat or drink any milk product, nothing with even the tiniest amount of cow's milk in it. After five days of this maternal diet change, the rash disappeared and there was some improvement in the vomiting and colic.

Maisy was prescribed omeprazole and maternal cow's milk avoidance was continued. By 6 weeks old, the colic had disappeared but Maisy was still vomiting, up to three times per feed. There was some discomfort and pain with the vomiting, but she was mostly a happy baby, and was growing and thriving.

By the time she was three months old she had no discomfort or rash, she was growing well and her stools were normal. Vomiting though had worsened, up to four to five times per feed. The omeprazole was increased to the maximum dose.

Two weeks later, believing that Maisy was uncomfortable on the higher dose of omeprazole the drug was stopped for five days. The vomiting considerably worsened. When the omeprazole was restarted the vomiting dramatically improved.

Maisy's vomiting and discomfort had made breastfeeding a challenge and Mother wanted to transition to formula feeding. Following a single feed of Enfamil AR Maisy had severe colicky symptoms, worse vomiting and scratched her abdomen for several hours.

Parents and Maisy went on holiday and Mother experimented with different formula feeds. Maisy constantly cried, so much so that parents abandoned their holiday. Maisy then switched to formula feeding with Aptamil Pepti, an extensively hydrolysed cow's milk formula (eHF).

A combination of Aptamil Pepti and omeprazole finally controlled the crying, colic and vomiting. The diagnosis was non-IgE-mediated, slow onset, cow's milk allergy and gastroesophageal reflux.

Carl

At six weeks old Carl started excessively crying – the crying occurred for most of the day and for an hour after every feed at night. The crying occurred with feeding, did not escalate towards the evening, and was associated with severe vomiting. By the time Carl was four months old Mother was desperate. There was no bile or blood in the vomits and the stools were normal. Carl was solely breast fed and was thriving.

Carl had been prescribed dicycloverine and simethicone for colic, chlorpheniramine for itching and a faint, eczematous rash, and ompepazole for reflux. The first three drugs were not helpful in reducing symptoms but the vomiting improved modestly with omeprazole.

Carl was given Enfamil AR formula to help reflux. Within minutes he had an immediate severe allergic reaction with whole body florid rash and breathing difficulties, and was extremely fractious.

With this clear evidence of a reaction to formula feeding, Carl was solely fed with Aptamil Pepti and his symptoms (rash, crying and vomiting) all dramatically improved. The diagnosis was Ig-E-mediated fast-onset cow's milk allergy. Omeprazole was stopped two weeks later and he remains symptom-free on the eHF formula.

7. Trapped wind ('wind')

Wind is air in Baby's stomach, swallowed with feeding and crying.

Air can make the infant feel temporarily full even though not satiated and cause pain from overdistension. Baby may have a bluish perioral tinge, pull away from the breast or bottle and cry. If laid down Baby won't settle.

The air accumulates at the top of the stomach and is trapped above the inlet of the oesophageal sphincter. Releasing this air back into the oesophagus is the treatment. It sounds simple but in practice can be hard to achieve – patience and positioning are required until Baby 'burps'.

Positions

Three good burping positions are with Baby face down over your palm, over the lap, and over the shoulder. A common pattern of burping is the infant takes in about three quarters of the feed, burps successfully and then finishes what's left.

Upright feeding helps prevent wind. A breast-fed baby tends to be more upright than when bottle fed and wind is less of a problem. When bottle feeding the bottle should be tilted up, the milk always covers the teat outlet, reducing the amount of air drawn in with the milk.

Bottles

There are a variety of commercial bottles that permit air to enter through the base when the bottle is upright, such as Dr Brown or Mam. If the air can enter easily to replace the volume of milk consumed and less negative pressure is required to draw the milk from the bottle, then less air will be taken in with the feed. The stronger the suck required, the more likely air will be drawn in around the side of the teat.

Can't release the wind?

If Baby is getting irritable when burped, it may mean he or she wants to continue feeding and doesn't need to burp. At other times, the infant does have wind despite your efforts. A good rule of thumb is three to five minutes in three different positions should help produce a burp. If Baby does not burp, carry on feeding (as their crying may be ongoing hunger rather than wind) or try to settle Baby in other ways.

Do any medicines help?

Simethicone (Infacol) may work by encouraging gas bubbles to coalesce so that can then be expelled more easily by burping. Clinical trials have not convincingly shown it to work for wind or colic. Don't give it if your baby is hypothyroid and receiving thyroxine as medication.

8. Hunger and feeding difficulties

Breast feeding is natural but this doesn't mean it's easy. Mother and Baby are initially on a steep learning curve. Success is more likely if there is repeated breast-feeding tuition, including correction and re-correction of maternal baby positioning.

In England where breast feeding is strongly promoted, more than three quarters of women do so with the good intention of continuing for as long as Baby wants. Unfortunately only a quarter of mothers manage beyond six weeks.

This statistic attests to the challenges of breast feeding in modern times. Turning these figures around, a quarter of women go directly to formula feeding, which has an association with higher rates of wind, reflux and CMA. Three quarters are formula feeding by the time their babies are six weeks old. This is because breast feeding is difficult to master without support and Baby becomes increasingly frustrated and hungry.

A phenomenon is the baby who is not feeding well and is crying excessively from hunger. The infant may have green, loose stools and may not be thriving – possibly growing but slower than the trajectory of the centile they were born on.

What differentiates the hungry baby from those with CMA is the lack of mucous or blood in stools in the hungry baby, no rash and ability to settle when a feed goes well.

Babies with reflux can look as though they have feeding difficulties because they're in pain when feeding. They may pull on and off the breast, switching between pain and hunger. There are subtle differences in refluxing and hungry scenarios – refluxing babies have good attachment but pull away frequently; hungry babies have poor attachment from the outset. A lactation consultant will be good at identifying which problem your baby has. If it is 'hungry baby scenario' she'll help you establish a good feeding technique.

Fighting at the breast

Check Baby's position at the breast – most of the nipple and much of the areola should be inside Baby's mouth and the nose should be free of the breast (Baby's head should be tilted back slightly). Ensure Baby's nose is not blocked (use saline nasal spray and a nasal suction trap, or consult your family doctor or health visitor). Get Baby to suck on a dummy then switch quickly to the breast. Try different feeding positions (sitting up, lying down, baby side lying or vertical).

Express some milk before feeds if the breast is too hard at the start of feeding. Feed on one breast, changing sides at each feed for a few days. Feed more frequently if there is too little milk.

If you are still having difficulties visit a lactation consultant at your local midwifery/obstetric unit or consult a breast-feeding support group such as the La Leche League or National Childbirth Trust (NCT).

Breast feeding for many is not easy. It is a learnt skill and the technique will be better and more successful if done in partnership with an expert tutor.

9. Constipation

Babies' normal frequency of passing stools varies enormously from every feed to once every two days. A 'constipated' baby is one who appears uncomfortable when passing stools and whose stool frequency has changed significantly over a short period of time. Usually associated with commencing Gaviscon, feed thickener, a change to formula feeding from breast milk or change of type of formula. The discomfort from the straining and worsening of reflux both exacerbate crying.

The two main choices when dealing with a constipated baby are to revert to what you were doing before the constipation (stop or reduce the Gaviscon, thickener or new formula) or add something to increase the frequency of stools (water, fresh orange juice or lactulose).

Constipation management

- Usually associated with treatments for other causes of crying
- Constipation is not normally a feature in a breast-fed baby

First line: Stop or reduce Gaviscon or thickener

Second line: Reconsider the diagnosis. There may be something more serious – think of Hirschsprung's and hypothyroidism

Third line: Treatments for constipation
- cooled boiled water
- fresh orange juice
- lactulose

10. Lactose intolerance

Lactose is the main carbohydrate in human milk, accounting for about 5 percent of the total constituents. It is broken down in the small intestine into two absorbable sugars – glucose and galactose – by the enzyme lactase. Lactulose, used to treat constipation, is not the same as lactose.

Lactose itself is not directly absorbed by the gut and if not broken down in the small intestine, is fermented by bacteria in the colon to release CO_2, methane and hydrogen. These in turn cause the symptoms of lactose intolerance.

Primary lactose intolerance is the most common genetic condition in the world. Although crying is commonly blamed on lactose intolerance in fact it only rarely causes symptoms in babies. For those who have primary lactose intolerance, the onset of symptoms appears to be from two years old onwards. This is because the common genetic defect produces a reduction but not complete absence of lactase. This reduced enzyme condition is compensated for in babies, because they have higher expression of the lactase gene – hence more lactase for the first two years of life. This is a natural phenomenon selected to cope with the increased lactose in babies' milk-based diet.

Enzyme levels naturally decline around two years old, when those with this 'relative' deficiency of lactase become symptomatic. This condition usually runs in families and has a greater preponderance in certain racial groups, including Asian. It can be so common, most of the population have it, and so is considered a variant rather than a disease.

There is also a rare form of lactose intolerance where there is total absence of gut lactase and no lactose breakdown at all, even in babies. This condition presents with severe watery diarrhoea in the first few days of life. Virtually no baby with excessive crying or colic will have this condition.

It is possible that some babies have relatively immature lactase enzyme systems in their small intestine or have secondary lactase deficiency after a viral infection. Theoretically, the notion that lactose intolerance is a major cause of crying in babies is popular and many commercial formulas are now lactase treated to give low levels of lactose. Evidence to support the idea that lactose intolerance is a real cause of crying in babies is, however, missing. Trials of lactase pre-treatment of milk for colic or excessive crying do not show convincing results and such babies do not have undigested lactose in their stools.

In spite of the lack of evidence, lactase drops (Colief) are cheap, and a short trial to see if they reduce crying seems reasonable. If Baby is already formula fed, an easier option than pre-treating your own milk is switching to a low-lactose/lactose-free formula, such as SMA Comfort. Some ex-premature babies have developmental lactase deficiency which usually improves with age. These babies may respond well to lactase enzyme supplementation or milk treatment.

> **Low lactose and lactose-free formulas**
> - SMA Lactose Free
> - Enfamil O-Lac

11. Experimental approach to treating crying when the diagnosis is uncertain

The specific cause of excessive crying is often not obvious. The algorithm shown below may be beneficial if the diagnosis is uncertain.

Crying where the diagnosis is uncertain

- Focus on good winding and feeding techniques
- Consider simethicone, lactase drops and herbal tea
- If already formula feeding, try a commercial colic milk such as partially hydrolysed and lactose-reduced

If vomiting or frequent posseting

Level 1: Gaviscon or thickener and ranitidine

Level 2: Maternal complete avoidance of CMP, if breast feeding

eHF, if formula fed

Level 3: PPI (omeprazole, then esomeprazole or lansoprazole.

Early weaning if older than four months

Level 4: Add in domperidone if convinced you're dealing with reflux

If no vomiting

Level 1   Probiotics

Level 2   Maternal complete avoidance of CMP, if breast fed

eHF, if formula fed

Level 3   Trial of soya-based milk

- Not usually beneficial to step up to AAF, unless there is convincing evidence of severe CMA (especially IgE-mediated)

- Probiotics – consider using a lower dose than recommended on the packet. Stop if vomiting or a rash occurs.

PART IV
Serious problems

The first thing to ask when faced with a high-pitched screaming and inconsolable baby is 'Could it be serious?' Even if you're confident you have a healthy baby, a visit to a family doctor or paediatrician can be reassuring. This will help allay fears in the middle of the night when you're exhausted and not thinking straight.

12. Signs of serious illness

Seek medical attention as soon as you can if your baby

- has a weak, high-pitched continuous cry
- seems floppy when picked up
- has shallow, weak breathing
- is pale or shocked when crying (red and angry goes with colic)

- takes less than a third of their usual daily amount of milk
- passes much less urine than usual
- has green vomits (bile)
- consistently forceful vomiting (projectile vomiting which hits the shoes of someone standing close by) could mean pyloric stenosis which presents in a first-born, male baby between two to six weeks old (especially likely if mother had the condition as a baby)
- passes blood in their stools
- has a fever of 38°C or above (if they're less than three months old) or 39°C or above (if they're between three and six months). This does not apply in the day or two after the MenB vaccine.
- has a high temperature but hands and feet feel cold
- has a bulging fontanelle (the soft spot on a baby's head) and appears unwell or floppy. Many healthy babies have a raised fontanelle when crying, so this sign is not good for differentiating well from unwell babies
- has a fit
- turns blue, mottled or very pale
- has a stiff neck
- has difficulty breathing. Breathes fast or grunts, or seems to be working hard to breathe (drawing in of the ribs in the lower chest)
- has a spotty, purple-red rash anywhere on the body (this could be a sign of meningococcal disease)

- has abdominal tenderness and/or distension
- has recurrent pneumonia
- has weight loss or failure to thrive

PART V

What to do if your baby doesn't respond to treatment

When Baby doesn't respond to treatment, or while waiting to see if a particular management pathway will work there are two approaches – calming and soothing techniques and parental coping strategies.

13. Calming and soothing techniques

Different comforting techniques work with some babies but not others. The best approach is to try one technique for a short period of a few minutes and if it works, continue. If it doesn't, switch techniques.

Parents can a take turns to comfort Baby, giving each a break from incessant crying.

Colic doesn't occur in some racial groups and societies which have a culture of carrying babies all the time. This absence of colic may or may not be related to the constant carrying.

When soothing techniques are subjected to clinical trials in persistently crying Caucasian babies, reducing stimulation seems to be more effective than increased carrying. See what works best for your baby. Here are some suggestions.

- **Don't forget to do the simple things and check the baby is comfortable** – clothes not too tight; not too hot or cold (feel the back of the neck or the tummy to gauge temperature); change the nappy; try different nappies; let Baby kick, nappy-free; treat any nappy rash and check for clothing rashes.

- **Hold and swaddle Baby during crying episode** – wrap Baby snugly in a blanket or baby sling.

- **Hold Baby in different positions** – on your shoulder, cradled in your arms, lying with the tummy face down along your forearm (leopard position).

- **Sit or hold Baby upright during feeding – to prevent air swallowing.**

- **Avoid overstimulating by continually picking up and putting down – gently comforting your** baby in a quiet, darkened room may be better. If you're satisfied Baby isn't hungry, tired, too hot or cold or in need of a nappy change, it may help to leave the infant in the cot for a while even if it continues to cry (some babies need to cry a little as part of their falling to sleep routine). Reduce stimulation by not patting, lifting and jiggling. Reduce environmental noise.

- **Movement** – rhythmic movement often settles a baby. Gentle rocking in a pram or over a shoulder is hypnotic. Pushing Baby around in its pram or pushchair is comforting. Be careful to rock but not shake Baby.

- **White noise** – this is the background sound of a washing machine, vacuum cleaner, radio static or app on a smartphone.

- **Gentle stomach or back rubs or a warm bath** – may help.

- **Offer breast, bottle or dummy (pacifier).**

- **Take Baby for a ride in the car** – but don't drive if you are exhausted.

- **Change the scenery but avoid overstimulation**.

- **Physical comfort** – babies need to adjust to not being in the womb. They need to be held warm and close to know someone is nearby (the fourth trimester scenario).

- **Establish a getting to sleep pattern** – in a bedroom which is quiet and dark. Baby begins to associate the place to sleep with calmness.

- **Sometimes Baby is tired but fighting sleep** – don't be afraid to put Baby down somewhere safe to cry for a short time. Some babies need to settle themselves.

- **Some babies are more sensitive** – handle and talk gently and quietly, keep up a routine, limit visitors and don't pass Baby between lots of people.

- **Visit a cranial osteopath** – to reassure yourself.
- **Baby slings** – these provide movement and comfort.
- **Some babies prefer the dark** – others like low light at night.
- **Help Baby find a thumb to suck** – for comfort.
- **Use time away from Baby to look after yourself** – have a bath, eat well and relax.

14. Parental coping strategies

Talking to relatives, friends and other parents is a vital part of coping. It may seem impossible to leave the house to visit friends or attend a baby support group when you are exhausted. But not getting out intensifies a sense of isolation and makes it easy to believe you're the only one with difficulties.

Others may have some ideas you've not thought of or simply reassure you things will get better and you're doing a good job. Even if they can't help it may be a relief to simply get things off your chest.

You may need time away from your baby. Get your partner, a grandparent, close relative or friend to look after Baby while you take a break. This may be for a few hours, overnight or for a day or so.

Bottles of expressed milk or formula can make a big difference to your ability to cope.

Sometimes it's necessary to put Baby down in a safe place, walk out of the room, shut the door and take a short break. If there is no serious illness and your nerves are at breaking point, do this to give yourself time to relax.

Talking to your partner and being frank about how you are feeling is an essential part of coping.

Apportion no blame and feel no guilt in asking for help. Take turns to hold your crying baby and be awake, together at times, during the sleepless nights.

If sleep deprivation is an issue, sleep separately for

a while, one partner on the sofa or spare bed, for at least part of the night. Alternate so you both get patches of quality sleep.

Create a sanctuary in the house if possible – a spare room away from the crying to escape to when your partner is with your baby.

Usually mothers develop different coping strategies to fathers, a reflection of variations in parental character. It may also be Baby demands it, each parent having a different smell, feel and aura. So when you see your partner doing something you feel won't work or think you know better, hold back for a while to see what happens. In early months much of the time is about getting to know each other. Baby will learn to behave differently with each parent. Don't fall into the trap of feeling you're the only one who can settle Baby. Don't take the whole burden of the crying baby on yourself, blocking out your partner.

Another catch is parents start blaming each other for not settling Baby. Remember the crying is no one's fault and you're both doing your best.

If the father returns to work after a short period, the mother will spend more time with Baby and acquire better skills at interpreting the cues as to what Baby wants. Mothers may also intuitively better understand a baby's needs in this early phase.

Society is changing though and in some partnerships mother will return to work quickly and father spend more time at home in the first year. Whatever the case, it's important to keep in mind the other parent must have space and time to reach the same level of understanding.

If you see your partner making mistakes you've already made, try positive, gentle suggestions to help reach a better understanding of Baby. Try to have a hands-off approach.

If exhausted and you find it unbearable to see your partner struggling to settle Baby, when you feel you know exactly what to do, it may be better to leave the situation rather than take over. Don't feel guilty about escaping – to go to a quiet bedroom for a snooze or have a coffee with a neighbour. Even when you know you can do a better job, taking over reduces the learning experience of your partner. They become less capable and this ultimately adds to exhaustion and resentment because the burden of settling Baby falls on you.

Talk to your health visitor or family doctor about how the crying is affecting you. Get help from them if you need it. Be aware of the signs of early postnatal depression or simply low mood – in both parents. Use a depression scale such as Hamilton (www.psy-world.com/online_hamd.htm) if you are concerned about your mood being low. Try meditation (www.headspace.com) when Baby is asleep.

There are some excellent internet resources to be used in conjunction with this book – Cry-sis (www.cry-sis.org.uk) and The National Childbirth Trust (www.nct.org.uk/parenting/coping-crying-baby).

Printed in Great Britain
by Amazon